Forest
Folk Tales
for children

To

Amber + Jacob,

Enjoy the stories,

Forest Folk Tales

for children

Tom Phillips

Illustrated by Amanda Vigor

The
History
Press

First published 2019

The History Press
The Mill, Brimscombe Port
Stroud, Gloucestershire, GL5 2QG
www.thehistorypress.co.uk

Text © Tom Phillips, 2019
Illustrations © Amanda Vigor, 2019

The right of Tom Phillips to be identified as the Author
of this work has been asserted in accordance with the
Copyright, Designs and Patents Act 1988.

British Library Cataloguing in Publication Data.
A catalogue record for this book is available from the British Library.

ISBN 978 0 7509 9141 4

Typesetting and origination by The History Press
Printed and bound in Europe by Imak

Contents

Introduction

Who am I?

Firstly, let me introduce myself and thank you for buying my book. I am Tom Phillips, formally known as Mr Phillips when I was a primary school teacher, sometimes known as Tom the Tale Teller when I travel the lands telling traditional stories, folk tales, myths and legends to audiences of children and adults alike as a storyteller, and most of the time I'm known as Daddy by my two young children who both love stories and adventures in the countryside.

Why did I write this book?

I grew up in a sleepy little village in Leicestershire. We didn't have a forest or large woodland nearby, but we did have lots of spinneys and hedgerows full of trees. I must have climbed (or tried to climb) every tree in my village growing up. I loved trees and nature (despite having hay fever and actually being allergic to tree pollen, it never stopped me). I remember stopping off for picnics in the Forest of Dean on our way to our family holidays in Pembrokeshire every year and being amazed by the number of trees in this forest. I have always found forests and woodlands magical places to explore and, when I became a storyteller and writer, I discovered all this folklore surrounding these mystical places. I have also started working deep within the National Forest and so thought now was the best time to write this book.

How have I written it?

I used books to help me find the stories. Most of the time they were short little nuggets which I have had to stretch out and shape to make them the enjoyable stories I knew they could be. I would write the book out, read it over, change what I needed, then give it to Samantha, my wife, to proofread it before testing it on Emelia, my daughter. The whole book was written in just over two months. It took a LOT of research and a LOT of work writing it up but, well, I am happy with how it turned out and hope you are too.

So, get reading, go get lost in the stories, learn something new and then go and explore the countryside and forests of this wonderful country, from Scotland to Wales and through the length and breadth of England, trying out some of the Why Don't You? suggestions and making up your own fun and games.

Enjoy!

Hobs

Yorkshire Forests
of Guisborough,
Dalby and the North
Yorkshire Moors

Hidden in your house or grounds,
Helping out all around,
Cleaning up or doing the milking,
Any jobs that might need doing,
They live to work, this they do,
Not for themselves, but all for you.
In return they ask for nought,
So leave them be, don't seek them out.
Let them alone, leave them be,
And a better home you'll have for thee.

Yorkshire is a land of extremes, from the lush, wooded valleys to the harsh, exposed moorland. The whole county just takes your breath away. And then, after travelling through the most amazing countryside, you reach the sea, a coastline of cliffs, harbours and fossils, hiding secrets from millions of years ago. Many years before, the moors were covered in trees with the great forests of Dalby to the south and Guisborough to the north, stretching as far as the sea to the east. Even now, the North Yorkshire Moors have more trees than the New Forest!

Many stories are told of this ancient landscape and the creatures and people who lived in it. One such story tells of a brave young man who slew a dragon, but alas, there is not room for his story in this chapter.

We shall be hearing about hobs. Now I'm guessing you thought I meant to write hobgoblin. Well, I didn't but they wouldn't be far off what I'm talking about. You may recognise hobs as something else though. The great J.K. Rowling used hobs in her Harry Potter stories, but she did not call them by that name. She named them house elves.

Hobs are thought to be little men that live in your house. They are only a few feet high, about the size of a toddler, and often have a long beard that brushes the floor as they walk. They do not wear clothes and have a large nose that takes up most of their face. These funny little creatures are rarely seen, but what they do can be very easily spotted.

Hobs are thought to be extremely helpful little things. They work on the land, helping the farmer, or live in local caves, looking out for the people of the nearby village. All they need in return is to be left alone and respected. However, if you upset one, disrespect him or anger him in some way, he will become naughty and mischievous, causing bad things to happen on your farm. The only way to get rid of a hob is to give it a new set of clothing to wear. With this, most of them leave the house and don't come back, but not all. Some, in really bad cases, never leave and even follow you if you move!

There are not many girl hobs but it is believed that there are some. These are mostly called hobthrusts and live in wooded areas and in forests.

Lots of these funny little creatures were given names, names that would make us giggle such as:

Hodge Hob O'Bransdale,
Robin Round-Cap of Spaldington,
Old Delph Will of Saddleworth,
Elphi Bandy Legs of Low Farndale.

The Hob of Hart Hall

Hart Hall stands amongst trees and moorland on the edge of Guisborough Forest, not far from Whitby. It was said that many, many years ago, the farmers who worked the land were gifted by the help of a hob. The story goes like this …

Once, there lived a hob on the farm at Hart Hall. He was rarely seen by any of the farm workers but they all knew he was there. At night, after the farm workers had filled the barn with the harvested wheat and grain, the hob would appear to thresh them until the moon became sleepy and the sun rose from his slumber. By threshing them, the hob separated the grain from the rest of the plant, ready for the grain to be gathered up and made into flour, beer or any of the other many foodstuffs you could make from cereal crops. The hob would do twice as much in one night as a single person and could finish the whole barn before dawn. With the hob's help, the farmer made a good living and never had to hire many workers, so he didn't have to pay too many people.

However, one night, after the sun had slipped beneath the hills in the west, the youngest of the farm workers was feeling curious. He had heard the stories of the hob and was keen to find out what this creature actually looked like. He wanted to see it with his own eyes. Slipping from shadow to shadow like a ninja farmer, the boy made his way to the threshing barn. Finding a gap in the wooden boards of the barn walls, the curious boy peered a single eye through. Lo and behold, there was the hob.

The boy watched and saw the hob, threshing the crop at such speed that the flails in his hands were a blur. He wielded two at once and had such skill as to never hit them together by accident. It was a marvel to watch. However, it was then that the boy noticed the size of the hob. He was tiny! No bigger in height than the shoulder of the sheep on the farm. The boy also noticed something that made him withdraw with shock. What at first he thought was some kind of fur coat was actually a mixture of the hob's long beard and body hair. The hob was NAKED!

The boy, shocked at first, then took pity on the poor creature. He must be cold, even with all that hair, he thought. The boy had an idea. He returned to his work colleagues and told them of what he saw. They too took pity and it was decided that they were to give him some clothes. During the next day, some of the farm workers gathered some scraps of fabric and stitched them together to make a simple tunic, known as a hamp. Before the sun had set, they left it in the threshing barn so that the hob would find it, and then they hid, so they could see what happened.

They were all very excited. Surely the hob would love his present! If he did the job of two men when naked, he could do the job of four men if he was warm and clothed, they thought. As they were congratulating themselves and waiting, into the barn walked the hob.

The hob walked up to the clothing, picked it up and screamed in anger. The onlookers were very confused. The fury of the hob could be seen written all over his face. He then spoke, in a voice like rocks tumbling onto the ground, and said, 'Gin hob mun hae nowght but a hardin' hamp, he'll coom nae mair, nowther to berry nor stamp.'

But what does this mean? You may well ask as this is old speech and needs some deciphering. Let me help.

'Gin hob mun hae nowght but a hardin' hamp' means 'give the hob man nothing but a hard hamp' (we know what hamp means, remember?).

'He'll coom nae mair, nowther to berry nor stamp' means 'he will come no more, never to berry or stamp (thresh the grain)'.

The hob, like all hobs, liked being naked. They were born that way and lived their whole life that way. Maybe he would have accepted a nice outfit, a smart suit, but what he was being given was a hamp. This was a type of tunic worn by a farm worker. The hob really did not like being thought of as just a farm worker. He felt he was so much more – after all, he could do twice as much in one night as any other farm worker. And with that, the hob disappeared, never to be seen again.

It was the next morning when, pushed by the others, the young farm worker who had started all of this told the farmer what had happened. The farmer was fuming. He knew of hobs and knew you never give them clothes as this will drive them away. Now the farmer had to pay for more workers and those workers he had needed to work extra hard. In the end, the farm failed – all because a young boy wanted to help a hob.

Hob Hill

Further north, on the top side of Guisborough Forest, there was once a farmer by the name of Oughtred who, much like in the last story, had a helpful hob. However, this time what happened was purely by accident.

One day, one of the workers left his coat on a piece of machinery. When the hob arrived to help that night, he found the coat and was not happy. As we know, you should never give a hob any clothing. However, unlike in the last story, the hob didn't leave; he decided to get even. It was then it started.

Over the next few weeks, strange things began to happen. Bottles where pushed off shelves and broken, the cattle were let loose from their barn, and the freshly separated grain and chaff were mixed together again, so they had to be sorted once more. This lasted for a month with the farmer trying everything. He knew what had happened, he knew it was a mistake and tried his hardest to get the hob to listen to his apology, but it was no good. He couldn't see the hob.

In desperation, the farmer went to the wise man of the village for help. The only advice the wise man had was for the farmer and his family to move. The farmer managed eventually to sell the farm but for next to nothing. After all, who wanted to buy a farm plagued by a mischievous hob? Not me, that's for sure.

The day of the move came. The horse and cart were piled high with the farmer's family's belongings and they began to ride off down the lane. As the family sat at the front of the cart, a little hairy face popped out of the loaded cart, over the farmer's shoulder and said, 'We're we gahin ti flit ta?', meaning 'Where are we going to flit (go) to?'

There are many other stories of hobs, hobthrusts and hobmen from around Yorkshire and the midlands, from Staffordshire to Charnwood Forest in Leicestershire, some helpful, some mischievous, some a bit of both, but they all have one thing in common. These creatures can be very helpful but will leave if given clothes. So, if you find you have a hob, if chores get done as if by magic overnight in your house, maybe you have a hob! Because it wouldn't be your parents, cleaning up after you, would it? Just be sure you never give them clothes or else they'll be gone for ever.

DID YOU KNOW?

Hobs have also been called hobbits!
It is thought that they were the
inspiration for the hairy-footed stars
of J.R.R. Tolkien's *The Hobbit* and *Lord
of the Rings* books. Like the hobbits
of Middle Earth, there is a hob that
lives in a hole in the ground near
Runswick Bay. He is believed to be
able to cure whooping cough and
many people from the local village
have been to this creature's cave to
cure themselves or their children of
this terrible illness.

WHY DON'T YOU?

Clean your room! Well, let's be honest, it is very rare to have a helpful hob around the house, cleaning and tidying. Usually, that's done by mum, or dad, or whoever looks after you in your house. But maybe, if you keep your room clean, they might reward you with some new clothes or, even better, a day out to your nearby forest where you can explore, play and have adventures, keeping an eye out for the wondrous things you find in this book. Give it a go – clean your room and see what it gets you.

Dragons

Forests of North Wales;
Beddgelert Forest,
Clwyd Forest and
Gwydir Forest

Swooping in the dark,
riding upon the moon's rays,
Leathery wings block the stars
and warn of the end of days,
The orange flame lights up the sky
and death is smelled by all around,
Down it swoops upon its foil,
there upon the ground.
Dagger teeth sink into the skin,
flesh tears open, meat consumed,
The village waits, a deadly silence now,
until by fire it is doomed.

Well, I can't rightly talk about folk tales from the Welsh forests without talking about the mighty dragon, can I now? The Welsh have a great, red dragon on their flag, so it makes sense for this to be the home of dragons in the British Isles. In the north of the country, it is barren and mountainous, with great forests sprawling across the hillsides, draping the valley floors with a giant cloak of emerald green.

Wales is also well known as the home of a famous legendary king, King Arthur himself. Many stories are told of his great doings, such as his defeat of the giant Rita Fawr on the summit of Snowdon. However, we will not be hearing of these. I will be telling you of Arthur's most trusted and most powerful friend, the wizard Merlin, as he had something to do with a dragon or two.

Vortigern and the Dragons

When Merlin was young, he lived near the village of Beddgelert in around the fifth century. Nearby, the king at the time, a vile, mean man by the name of Vortigern, was trying to build his seat of power, a mighty castle that would stand on an upturned bowl-shaped hill, looking out across the land. This fort was to be impenetrable, the strongest castle ever to have been built. He drafted in the finest architects and the most skilled builders in the land, but there was a problem. It seemed that no matter how firm or how deep the foundations were laid, the castle would crumble down before it was completed. Time and time again they tried, but time and time again it crumbled.

Vortigern began to lose his temper. Before he started executing the builders, he asked his soothsayers (fortune tellers of a sort) to tell him how he could make this fort stand. They all agreed that the mortar for the foundations had to be mixed with the blood of a man with no natural father. As luck would have it, down the road lived Merlin. It was well known that he had no father and people thought, due to his magic, his father must have been a daemon. He was the man they needed; his blood would help the castle stand.

So it was that Merlin found himself in front of Vortigern, a knife at his throat, pleading for his life. Merlin was still young at the time but he had wisdom beyond his age. He did not break down and cry. Instead, he spoke calmly.

'These men know not of what they are talking,' he said, and he waved a hand toward the soothsayers, 'for I have seen why the castle will not stand. Listen to my words, take my advice, spare my life and I will ensure your fort stands for many years to come, strong and firm, just as you do as our leader.' This was smart as Vortigern was vain and loved himself. Merlin knew this and made him feel special.

Vortigern agreed to give Merlin a chance. He had heard of his power and so released him. Merlin led the king to the hill and showed him a small crack in the cliff where a trickle of water leaked through. He ordered the builders to open the rock at that point. When they did, it released a great flood of water from a hidden lake. The water tore open the crack where the builders were standing. Out of the now gaping hole in the cliff face erupted two dragons, woken from a century-long slumber. One white, one red, the magnificent beasts tumbled out as one. They were locked in battle, teeth and claws, gnashing and slashing. Vortigern, Merlin, the soothsayers and the builders watched in awe.

As the dragons fought, the white dragon pinned the red one to the ground. His great claws tore flesh from bone and his teeth bit hard and deep into the red dragon's flanks. The red dragon refused to give in, instead flailing all four claws whilst on his back, much like a pinned cat. By doing this he began to tear the skin of the white dragon, causing his blood to stain his white hide crimson red.

Suddenly, with one mighty effort, the red dragon managed to flip the fight into reverse, rolling from underneath and pinning the white dragon down. Now it was the turn of the massive maroon monster to take his revenge. After what seemed like hours of the red dragon slashing and biting, the white dragon, close to death, and almost totally covered in blood, managed to free himself, opened his great wings and took flight towards the east.

The red dragon clawed his way up to the top of the hill where he stood proud, roaring to the heavens, breathing a great plume of smoke and flame towards the sky. With that, he too took flight, heading south.

'That,' said Merlin, 'is why your fort would not stand – the sleeping dragons would not let it.'

'But why did they fight?' asked Vortigern, still in shock and awe.

Merlin began to explain that this was a prophecy, a foretelling of the future. The white dragon represented the Saxons coming from foreign shores in the east, to invade the land of Vortigern and the Welsh. The red dragon was the ancient symbol of the Welsh. The battle showed that the Saxons would begin to win, that the battle would, for some time, seem lost, but that the Welsh would never give in, eventually turning the tide of battle and driving the Saxons from these shores.

Of course, Merlin was right. The castle could now be completed and it stood for many, many years. The Saxons came and were eventually driven away and, well, the rest of Merlin and Arthur's story is well known. Vortigern renamed the hill and the fort Dinas Emrys, after Merlin whose Welsh name was Myrddin Emrys.

In Wales, dragons go by another name, *gwiber*, which means both 'dragon' and 'viper' in Welsh. The Welsh folk believe that a dragon, or gwiber, is made when a viper snake drinks the milk of a human mother. As you can imagine, this would be a very hard thing to happen, which is why there are so few around. However, if it did happen, the viper would grow in size, grow four legs and two wings, be able to breath fire and still be venomous, like the viper it once was.

The Dragon of Denbigh

In the great forest of Clwyd there were many snakes – many vipers that bit many people, and many would die from these bites. There was one, however, that had somehow come across the milk of a human mother, drunk it and was now a much feared gwiber. This dragon had taken up home in a tumble-down old castle, coming out only to eat cattle or the occasional person. This was not liked by the people of the nearby village and they looked for someone brave enough to kill the foul beast.

The obvious choice was Sir John of the Thumbs. An odd name you may think, but he had an odd deformity that nobody else possessed. Sir John had two thumbs on each hand, giving him a total of twelve fingers (four thumbs in total), hence the name. The people thought that if the man had four thumbs he must be special, meant for greatness, and so he would be their champion.

Sir John was not a brave man and he was not particularly skilled in combat either, but he found himself without a choice. The villagers came to him, angered and upset at the dragon's presence. They demanded that Sir John take on the beast. With a crowd baying at his back he had two choices: take on the dragon and get killed in combat, or stay in the village and get killed by the villagers for being a coward. Alas, he decided it was better to die a hero than a coward and so, in his finest armour and with a lance at his side, Sir John mounted his horse and rode to the castle, the villagers singing his name as he left.

By the time he approached the remains of the once-great castle and its imposing gates, he was trembling from his head to his toes. The dragon mounted the arch of the gate, before dropping to the ground in front of the knight. He took one look at the man and began to laugh. He laughed so hard, the ground shook.

'They sent you, and only you?' the gwiber mocked.

It was then that he saw the knight's peculiar finger arrangement. Four thumbs?! The dragon had never seen or heard of such a thing. This made him laugh even harder! But that was the chance Sir John needed. He lowered his lance and charged. As the dragon threw his head back in laughter, Sir John's lance found the centre of his chest. The speed of the charging horse meant the lance sank deep into the dragon's heart and brought its beating to a stop. When the dragon had fallen to the floor, to make sure he was dead, the knight drew his sword and hacked off his head, which he took back to the village to prove what he had done.

'Dim bych!' the locals cried, 'Dim bych!' which in English means 'No more dragon'. And so it was, the village had been saved by a man with four thumbs. It was renamed Dimbych, which slowly over time became Denbigh, meaning 'no more dragon'.

Now, we often hear of the great deeds of knights defeating fearsome dragons and returning as heroes. But this is not always the case. Sometimes the hero does not return. Sometimes things go wrong. Let this next story be a warning for you …

The Gwiber of Penmachno

Deep in the Gwydir forest that wraps around the east side of Mount Snowdon and up towards Betws-y-Coed, there was once a great gwiber. He had grown to a great size, sprouted wings and was a plague on the land. The great beast had also decided he was going to live for ever.

Of course, up stepped a hero, an outlaw from Hiraethog, who felt it would massively help his reputation if he ridded the land of this creature. However, our hero was not daft. He was a wanted outlaw for a reason and that was because he had never been caught. He knew he needed a plan before confronting the dragon, so he sought advice from the local wise man. He asked him if, and how, he was going to die. The wise man told him he would be poisoned by the great beast.

Not satisfied by his first answer, after a night of going over and over the battle to come in his head, he decided to ask the wise man a second time. This time the wise man told the man he would die from a broken neck.

The man returned a third time to the wise man, knowing that if this time the answer was different, then he could disregard what the wise man said, as he clearly had no idea what he was talking about and truly had no power to see the future. And so it was that the third time the wise man told the outlaw he would drown.

Nonsense and poppycock, surely, thought the outlaw. How could he die in three different ways?! With this he set off to face the gwiber. The dragon lived high on a cliff above a river. The outlaw climbed up the cliff-face, for the dragon would never expect danger to come from this way. Who would be crazy enough to attack by climbing a cliff?

Upon emerging on the top of the cliff, the outlaw was met by a waiting dragon. He had heard the man climbing and lay in wait. A mouth full of teeth lunged at the man and bit him in the leg. The viper's venom sank into his bloodstream and the pain shot up his back.

He stumbled backwards, falling from the top of the cliff and tumbling down, striking his neck upon a rock as he fell before plummeting into the raging waters of the river below. And lo and behold, the outlaw was poisoned, his neck was broken and he finally drowned. The wise man was right. Wise men always are … unless a wise woman says otherwise, as a woman is always right – just ask your mum.

DID YOU KNOW?

Wales has a rainforest! Not all rainforests are in tropical areas. To the south of Maentrog in the Blaenau Ffestiniog area lies the rainforest of Llennyrch. Ceunant Llennyrch National Nature Reserve is an area of deciduous trees (they lose their leaves in autumn) which is constantly moist, so ferns and moss grow all year round.

WHY DON'T YOU?

Fight a log dragon. Find a large log in the forest and pretend it's a dragon. Try to fight it with your friends using sticks as swords. Remember, though, you need to work together to overcome this foul beast, not hit each other with your swords. Team work is key! Once you've defeated the giant worm, jump on his back and take him for a ride, soaring through the sky, in and out of the clouds!

Faeries

The Many Forests of Scotland and the Borderlands

Fair the faery folk they be,
Dancing around the ancient tree,
Singing songs of them and thee,
But never will they let you see.
Heed my words, stay away,
Let the fair folk at their play,
Life will be better, this I say,
If you walk away this day.
But if you must or if you need,
Talk to them, then this, please heed,
Please be sure that your deed,
Be one of kindness and not greed,
For then the faeries will be kind,
And hold thee with great regard in mind,
The rest of your life you will find,
The bad times are well left behind.

Scotland is one of the world's greatest natural wildernesses. The hills of the lowlands are carpeted in great pine forests, while the mountains of the highlands reach up from the woodlands and burst through the clouds above. From the ancient forest of Kielder on the Scottish border, across to the massive Gallaway forest, up past the Whitelee forest in Lanarkshire and on to Tay forest on the edge of the Cairngorns, to name but a few, forests are as much a part of Scotland as the hills and mountains.

These forests are said to be home to many wondrous creatures from mythical beasts to brownies – wee little men, very like the hobs of Yorkshire and the Midlands. However, the Scottish forests are famous for one legendary creature in particular – faeries!

Many, many stories have been told of the Scottish faery-folk, and these stories have inspired many artists. In fact, you already know a story with a Scottish faery in it. Do you know who Tinkerbell is?

'When the first baby laughed for the first time, its laugh broke into a thousand pieces, and they all went skipping about, and that was the beginning of fairies.'

J.M. Barrie was an author. He wrote the words you have just read in his most famous of books, *Peter Pan*. He was born in 1860 in Kirriemuir, Scotland, and grew up there before moving to London. Having grown up in Scotland, he had heard the stories of faeries and, well, it's no wonder these magical wonders found their way into his most famous of tales. To find out more about him you can visit his old house, now a museum in Kirriemuir, or the Peter Pan Moet Brae Trust in Dumfries – a magical place, well worth a visit.

So, J.M. Barrie knew about faeries and it's time you heard some stories about them too. Are you ready? Before we start, let me warn you, faeries are both nice and mischievous! Treat them well and they will reward you. Be mean or unkind to them and they will punish you, as you are about to find out.

Faery Friends

On the northern edges of the Kielder forest, just north of the ever-changing borderline of England and Scotland, lived a young farmer. He was a poor man with nought more than a tumble-down old house and a small field. He had been saving his money up all year long until the time had come for the end-of-year markets. He set off to market to buy himself a sheep. He would take it home, slaughter it to feed him through the long, cold winter months and sell the wool to make a bit more money. Not a single bit of that sheep would go to waste. It was all he could afford, so he had to make it last.

As he walked along on that somewhat grey day, he skirted the edge of a great pine forest. The wind blew chill and touched his bones, making him shiver and shake. He pulled his plaid, a tartan cloth worn by many in Scotland, around his shoulders and up to his chin, to try and keep warm. However, all of a sudden, off to his side, from a small clearing in the wood, the man heard a noise. He stopped and strained his ears to listen.

Voices drifted out of the glade but no people could be seen. The light was poor due to the thick cloud in the sky, but it was by no means dark. He should be able to see the people making the noise, he thought. Standing still, he listened again to the voices to see if he could make out what they were saying. At first, he could hear shouts of joy and much laughter. It sounded as if the unseen people were having a party, singing and dancing under a veil of invisibility.

But then he listened some more, straining his ears harder. That is when he discovered what the party was for – they were celebrating the birth of a wee bairn, a baby. But there was worry and sadness in some of the voices. They were calling for clothing or blankets. They were worried that the baby, still as naked as when it was born, would freeze in the cold and needed to be wrapped up.

The man had heard many stories when he was growing up about the unseen folk, those people who only show themselves when they want to be seen. These were faeries and no mistake! The man also knew it was best to steer clear of faeries as they were somewhat unpredictable, you never knew how they would treat you. That being said, the man could not simply ignore the naked, freezing child and walk on by, could he? Could you? What would you do?

Well, as you rightly guessed, and as I am sure you would do, the man decided to help. He unwrapped his plaid from his shoulders, laid it on the edge of the glade and stepped back. He watched in astonishment as invisible hands whisked the cloth away. He stayed for a moment longer to hear what happened. He heard the worried, scared voices become jolly and begin to sing with the rest, and his heart felt full of happiness.

The man set off once more, a smile on his face. It must have been the smile he wore that helped him at the market. He managed to get the biggest, woolliest sheep there for the lowest price of the day. What luck, he thought. However, after that day and every day thereafter, lucky things kept on happening. He had great wealth for the rest of his life, finally managing to move out of his small old house, to get married and to live, like in all good stories, happily ever after.

A Meal of Meal

Mrs Buckham lived not far from the man in the previous story, on the edge of the great forest. She lived on a farm and, come harvest time, her husband, family and farmhands began collecting in the year's hard work from the fields. It was still early in the harvest and barely any oatmeal had been collected, but Mrs Buckham needed to make dinner. As she was preparing to do this, into her house walked a small woman. She was no taller than the table and was dressed mostly in a beautiful woodland green with flashes of red here and there. Her face beamed brightly like the sun and Mrs Buckham noticed that her ears were pinched together at the top to give them a pointed look.

'I would very much like some meal to feed my family. Would you be able to spare some for us?' said the little lady in a soft, high-pitched voice.

Mrs Buckham knew at once that this woman was a faery, and she knew she must take care not to incur her anger. Giving a nervous little curtsey, as if in the presence of royalty, Mrs Buckham handed over the entire contents of the meal bowl and insisted the faery take it all.

The faery simply smiled, accepted the offer and left.

The very next day, the faery lady returned. She had brought with her the same amount of meal as Mrs Buckham had given her. This was put in the container and Mrs Buckham thanked the faery very much before she left.

Well, wouldn't you know, that meal, only being a small quantity, no more than a few handfuls, never seemed to reduce in size. Mrs Buckham made meal after meal for weeks and weeks until well after the harvest and into the winter, when it finally did, all of a sudden, run out. This was no problem, though, as Mrs Buckham still had the harvest, which hadn't been touched.

From then on, if food was ever running short, the meal container always seemed to have enough in it for Mrs Buckham to make something for the whole family to eat. Magic!

The Faeries of Merlin's Craig

In the county of Lanarkshire, long ago, people would rely on fire to keep them warm through the bitterly cold winters. Wood they had plenty of, but they also had something better: peat. This is mud from the ground, mud made up of old trees and other plants that have disappeared into the ground over many, many years and sat there in a lot of water. The peat itself is like a giant wet sponge, but if dug up in clods and dried out, it can be burned on a fire. These clods of peat, these peat bricks, would burn for a very long time, and this was perfect to keep a fire going through a long, cold night.

So it was that there was a young man called John Smith. He had a wife and two wee bairns and lived in one of the many pine forests that sprinkled the lowlands, in between the peat bogs on higher ground. He worked for a local farmer as a farm hand and, one day, in the height of summer, when the peat was drying out and would dry out completely if cut from the ground, the farmer told John to go up to a place called Merlin's Craig to cut peat, enough to keep the farmer's fires smouldering throughout the winter.

John had heard of Merlin's Craig. He had heard stories that told of the time the great wizard himself had visited it, gifting that high place its name. But the stories never told of why he went there, other than the land round about was soaked, not only with water in the peat, but with magic, right down into the stone below. John was hesitant about digging peat from that place, but a job's a job, the farmer paid him, John had to do it.

After a short walk from lowland to high, John sank his spade for the first time, once, twice, three times then four, heaving the peat brick up and out of the ground, upside down, to sit in the sun and begin to dry. As he started on the second brick, around from the back of a large stone, the size of a cart, came a small woman. She, much like the woman from the last story, was unmistakably a faery. Dressed in a plaid skirt of many colours and a long-sleeved top of heather and green, she had the brightest of red hair, like fire, that exploded from her head in all directions. Her face shone; she had dimples on her cheeks and points on her ears, but her frown was rumpled and her eyes were aflame.

'OI!' she yelled, 'You be putting the roof of m' house back rit now m'laddy!'

John froze in fear and bemusement. The faery continued, 'That be the roof of our house, ya wee rascal. Put it back before you regret it, sonny!'

Seeing the little faery meant business and having heard many a story when he was a child, he heeded her warning and flipped the first brick back into the hole he had made, bowed down low, backed away and began apologising again and again.

The faery left, and once she was far enough away, John ran as fast as he could, back to the farmer. Out of breath, he began to explain to him what had happened and the warning that something bad would happen if he carried on.

'Eigh, what a load of rubbish!' scorned the farmer, 'I pay ya to work, not to listen ta empty threats from an angry wee lassie! Now get back up there and do some work before I make something bad happen to yous!'

With that, John picked up his shovel once more, and began to return to Merlin's Craig. He was sure this was a mistake but what could he do? He needed this job, he needed the money to buy food to feed his family. The farmer was his boss, so he had to do as he was told. With this conflict racing through his mind, he soon found himself back where he started.

He began by removing the still-loose first brick he had dug before. Once it was out, he began to look all around in fear of the faery's return. Nothing. No faery, no warning, nothing. Happy now that it was all just in his head, John continued to dig, dig, dig.

Life went on as normal for John. He'd dug enough peat for both the farmer and himself, so winter was not too cold for his family. Summer returned and, on the anniversary of that strange day at Merlin's Craig, John was leaving the farm to return home with a jug of fresh milk from the farmer, a reward for a good day's work. As the sun had been shining brightly all day and was now setting, the sky was ablaze with reds, oranges and yellows. John decided to walk home along the upland, not through the forest as normal. He watched the fiery sky with awe and wonder until, all of a sudden, he heard music.

He lowered his head to see where he was and, yes my friends, you've guessed it, he was back in that magical place, Merlin's Craig, but he was not alone. All around him were faery folk, encircling him, dancing and singing a merry old tune. John dipped his head and tried to run away, but every direction he went, the faeries would stop him. He found himself buffeted from one part of the joyous circle to another. The faeries were laughing and singing; he was not.

It was then that a fair young faery maiden took his hand. She looked him in the eye and smiled. His heart melted for she was a thing of pure beauty and innocence. Within a flash, he had forgotten about his wife and two young children back home and began to dance. Setting the jug down upon a rock, John spiralled around and around as the strange words to the song filled his head, which became dizzy with delight. The faery maiden and John whirled towards a large opening in the same rock from behind which the faery woman had appeared a year before, and into it they fell.

As his eyes adjusted, John marvelled at the wonder he beheld. In front of him was another kingdom, here beneath the land. Hundreds of faery folk, busying themselves with tasks, making clothes, distilling faery whisky, baking, every one of them masters at their craft and all singing as they worked. John's eyes grew wide with delight.

Then, without warning, there in front of him appeared an old familiar face. It was the faery woman from a year ago. She looked angry when she began to speak. 'I told ya you would pay for taking our roof. Now, you will never speak of what else you are about ta see.' And with that, I can tell you no more of the faery kingdom.

You see, John heard the crowing of the cockerel for the coming of dawn and felt as though he had awoken from a dream. He was outside his house, still holding the fresh milk. He shook his head to clear the haze before walking into his house. 'Darlin,' you will not believe what I've just seen …'

His words stuck in his throat. He was statue still, stunned into disbelief. There, in front of him was his home, looking mostly as it always had, but something wasn't right. It looked more lived in than ever before. Standing before him was his wife, as beautiful as ever but with a few more lines on her face, and older, wiser eyes looking back at John.

Either side of her stood a young man and young lassie. He took a minute to see who they were, but then it was clear. These were his children, only they were no longer children.

'Seven years, John! Seven years! Where have ya been?!' The words stumbled out of his wife's mouth and crept like bugs into John's ears. They wriggled and scratched in his head as he tried to make sense of them. It had to be true for his children were at least that much older, but he had only just left the farm. He had only been gone a night, dancing with the faeries. If it had been seven years then the milk would not still be fresh, he thought, but it was, as fresh as the moment it left the cow.

John looked at his family, they back at him. Tears of happiness and confusion rolled down their faces. Placing the jug on the table, John scooped his family in his arms and hugged them. He had paid the price for disturbing the faeries and not heeding their warning. He had lost seven years – the time it had taken for the grass and moss to grow back on the faeries' roof. To him, it was a blink of an eye, a short night of joviality, but for his family, it was seven years of not knowing where he was, even if he was still alive.

So, my friends, if you are out exploring the pine forests of Scotland, making memories and having adventures, be warned. The faery folk live there and they want nothing more than a peaceful life. Be careful what you do to the land around you, for it may be a faery's home and you do not want to be disturbing them. And be sure to remember your manners, should you be lucky enough to meet one. Help them out, share what you have and they will look after you in return.

DID YOU KNOW?

The way I have been spelling faery is the old-fashioned way. You will know the modern spelling, 'fairy'. This has become the way everyone seems to spell it nowadays but I like the old way. It can be spelled either with a 'y' at the end, as I have been spelling it, or an 'ie', but either way works. You can also use the old Norse symbol which joins up the 'a' and the 'e' to make 'æ'. It makes the word more interesting and it shows the faeries the respect they deserve. They have been around longer than any words, after all.

WHY DON'T YOU?

Make a faery house. Use twigs and leaves and any other materials you find in the forest to make a cosy little hideaway for our faery friends. Don't forget, they will need furniture, somewhere to sit, somewhere to sleep and somewhere to cook. Let your imagination fly. The more interesting and clever the house, the more the faeries will love it. Have fun!

Kings, Curses and Colluders

The New Forest, Hampshire

Noble of birth, never wanting,
their lives set out before thee.
The people of the land they rule,
but never truly see.
Blinded by privilege,
pleasure their only thought,
Living off their once great deeds
and the battles that they fought.
Carving up the land for their
own ill-gotten gains,
Those that stand against them
find themselves in chains.
But people plot and people plan,
to overthrow the crown,
To change the land, to change their
life and bring freedom to their town.

Don't be fooled by its name. The New Forest is far from new and not at all what you might expect a forest to be like. The New Forest is nearly one thousand years old! It was set up by William the Conqueror. You may have heard of him, the famous French king who came over to England and shot King Harold in the eye with an arrow (or one of his men did) during the Battle of Hastings. This produced the first ever comic book, the Bayeux Tapestry. If you have no idea what I am talking about, check it out!

Anyway, as I was saying, King William set up the New Forest as a hunting ground after he became king in 1066. He established forest law on the land. Forest law, William thought, was the perfect way of protecting the plants and animals of the forest. It was against the law to hunt any animal unless you were the king, with the king or had the permission of the king. Nobody could cut down trees, put up walls and fences, or keep dogs if they lived on this land. King William thought this was great and often hunted red deer, wild boar and hare in the forest. The locals were not so keen on the new law, for if they broke it, one of the punishments was to be blinded!

The Cursing of a King

When the New Forest was made, many homes were pulled down and many common people were made homeless. The king's guards would come to their houses, drag out the people living there and begin pulling down the houses, sometimes even burning them to the ground. All this just for the king to have his fun.

One day, the king's guards came to a little cottage on the edge of a thicket. Ivy and creepers grew around the door and the roof was thatched. Hanging from the door and window frames were shapes made of wood, sticks, feathers and fur. The men were hesitant to approach. They began chuntering among themselves, believing that a witch lived there. They all refused to pull down a witch's house.

The commander of the guards ordered them to stop speaking such nonsense and follow orders or else they would be put in jail or worse! So, they had no choice but to advance on the house, hoping nobody was in and that they could do the job and flee before the witch came back.

The commander knocked hard upon the heavy wooden door. As he waited for a response, all of a sudden, without it being touched, the door creaked open to reveal an old woman, dressed in strange clothing, hunched over a cauldron on the fire. 'Can I help you, deary?' croaked the woman. The commander could tell from her voice that she knew exactly why the guards were there and she was just humouring them.

'Men, do your duty, for the king!' bellowed the commander, waving the guards into the house. They did as they were told and flooded through the door. The old woman was dragged from the house kicking and screaming. The guards were all full of apologies. They kept saying how they didn't want to be doing this and it was all the king's fault.

'A curse!' screamed the old woman in a voice like nails down a chalkboard. 'A curse on the king, I cry!'

The men threw her to the floor and set the house ablaze, using burning logs that they had rolled out of the fire.

'The king will lose all of his sons, right here in this very forest. For this, the king's sons will die right here!' came the curse of the old woman.

The guards breathed a sigh of relief that the curse wasn't on them but on the king. Nobody really liked the king, not even his guards.

Well, was she a witch? Was her curse real? What I can tell you is that a short time later, Richard, King William's second son, was gored to death by a wild boar in the New Forest whilst out hunting and, well, this leads me onto my next story …

The Death of King Rufus

Rufus, or William II, became king after his father died in 1087. As a king, Rufus was not that different from his father. His father was mean and nasty to most people and a great warrior; so too was Rufus. He spent most of his time hunting rather than ruling the country. People of England were sick of having a ruler who did not care about them.

On 2 August 1100, King Rufus was out hunting with a group of his closest friends. The day was going well when a huge stag appeared. His antlers were like a mighty crown on his head as he stood tall and proud in a clearing, next to an ancient oak tree. The king saw the stag and began to draw his bow, but he was too slow. Walter Tirel, one of the king's closest friends and a fine shot with a bow, had already nocked an arrow and sent it flying through the air.

Now this, my friends, is where the story turns into a mystery and I will need you to read the facts and make your own minds up. So, Walter Tirel's arrow managed to find a chest, but not that of the deer, that of the king. The king fell from his horse to the ground, having been shot by his own friend. Then, for reasons we do not know, the people in the hunting party turned away and fled. Why? I don't know. Were they all in on a grizzly plot to murder the king, with Walter being the one to shoot him? Or did they all simply panic, not knowing what to do, and run away?

Some people say that it was an accident – that the arrow bounced off the nearby oak tree, missed its mark but found the king instead. This could have happened, as the deer was close to the tree and Walter, although being a great shot, was rushing to get his shot off before the king, a bit of healthy competition. His arrow could have been slightly off, brushing the tree and being deflected towards the unsuspecting king.

Let me tell you what happened next though, and then you can make up your mind. One of the men in the hunting party was Prince Henry, Rufus's youngest brother. When the king died, he rode hard north, towards Winchester, where he claimed the throne before his older brother, Robert, had the chance. Walter Tirel fled across the English Channel to France where he was safe. This all sounds very suspicious to me. What do you think?

No matter exactly what happened or the reason why, we do know the king's body was discovered later that day by a local poor man named Purkis. He took the body north to Winchester on the back of a cart, where Rufus was buried in the cathedral. It is said that the body dripped blood the whole way, a sign that the person had been murdered and that this was no accident. That is rumour and not a scientific way of working out how someone died, but, well, it is up to you.

Further to this, it is said that Walter Tirel stopped to wash his hands of the blood after pulling the arrow out of the king's chest. He did this in Ocknell pond, Lyndhurst, where it is said, even to this day, on the anniversary of this happening, the waters turn blood red.

Well, those are the facts as I know them, so it is up to you. Was the king murdered? Did his little brother get Walter Tirel to murder him so that Henry could be king? Or was it an accident? Hunting accidents were common – just look at what happened to Richard.

You decide …

Colluders to the Crown

Some 600 years after King Rufus died in that most suspicious of ways, more suspicious goings-on were afoot in the New Forest. King James II now sat on the throne and, as with most kings, there were many who sought to rebel against him. None more so than the Duke of Monmouth. He and his forces had suffered a crushing defeat in battle against the king and so, it was rumoured, the duke had fled to Lymington, to a large mansion now known as Monmouth House.

It was also said that the Duke of Monmouth had many supporters in that area who protected him. One such band of colluders (people who plot and plan to do something against the rules) met regularly in a nearby house. The house was owned by a kind elderly woman known as Mother Knapton. She would feed the men and let them discuss their plans, drawing them up and plotting in secret. However, news of their top-secret meetings leaked.

The king sent round a troop of guards one night, to catch them in the act. As the men pored over their plans, laid out on the table, and discussed the best way to overthrow the king, there came a knock at the door. They froze. Not a sound came out of their mouths as they listened and waited.

A deep, harsh voice boomed through the cracks in the door. 'Open up! We know you're in there and we know what you're up to!'

This was closely followed by thumping on the door as the guards tried to gain entry by force. Eventually, the door burst open and a group of well-armed men flooded in, filling the house. Greeting them was Mother Knapton, sitting alone with her back to them, staring into the fire, with the house otherwise empty. No sign of the colluders, other than a smell of beer and tobacco, the kind of smell you would expect in a tavern but not in a little old lady's house.

'Where are they?' screamed one of the guards at the old lady. 'I know they were here, I can smell their beer and tobacco!'

At that moment, Mother Knapton turned her head slowly. The king's men saw the old woman had a bandage wrapped around her head. What they didn't see were the papers with the plans on, hidden in the folds of the cloth.

'I'm terribly sorry, my dear,' she began, as cool as a cucumber, 'but I don't know what you mean.' Hanging from the corner of her mouth was a pipe and a tankard of ale was in her hand.

'You know what I mean, the smell, it's clear there were rebels here, men plotting against the crown!' The guard sounded less sure now, having seen the old woman.

Mother Knapton replied, 'Oh, the smell! I've got a terrible toothache, hence my head being wrapped up like so, and the tobacco and beer help numb the pain.'

The guard felt a bit foolish, so ordered the other guards to search the house. It didn't take them long and they found no trace of the men. They had slipped out of the back window as fast as lightning when the hammering on the door had begun and they were now a long, long way away, safe and sound.

DID YOU KNOW?

The New Forest was the first forest to be set up with forest law. The law was changed in 1217 so that people who owned land within the forest could set their livestock out to graze wherever they liked. This still happens today! The New Forest is famous for its ponies and cows that wander freely, across roads, through villages. If you are driving through the New Forest, keep an eye out for them.

WHY DON'T YOU?

Go on a hunt for the Rufus Stone. This stone is at the place where it is said King Rufus died. You can read about what happened and make up your own mind about what is the truth and what is a lie.

Ghostly
Beasts

Thetford Forest

On the wind, the howl, the growl,
From the shadow a smell so foul.
The hairs that sit upon your neck,
Stand on end and make you check,
Behind you first then all around,
Up in the tree and on the ground.
You're sure that something stalks you still,
So get out quick, from valley or hill,
For you they come, all teeth and claw,
The phantom beasts of legend and lore.

The great forest of Thetford is very new, although not the newest forest in this book. It was created after the First World War as so many of our trees had been cut down to make things for our armed forces during the war. The country needed wood, so this vast pine forest was planted. Evergreen pine trees are fast growing and so the forest sprang up in little over a decade (ten years). Before the forest, the land was barren, sandy and full of ridges and hollows, such as Grime's Graves. These aren't actually graves but pits where flint was mined long ago, during the Stone Age, to make weapons and tools. However, when the Vikings found them they thought them to be giant unused graves made by some kind of god, hence the name.

The land, being so sandy, was often affected by sand blows. These are like a sandstorm, where the wind picks up the sand and blows it about, making it very hard to see. Because of the sandy, soft land, another use for the area was as rabbit warrens, a place to almost farm rabbits, ready to catch them for the dinner table. And this is where my first story comes from.

The White Rabbit of Thetford

Life was good in Thetford. Trade was brisk for the traders, thanks to the town being on a main route to and from the east coast. Nearby stood a very imposing building. To look upon it you might think it was a castle or a fort, but you would be wrong. This was the house of the warrener. It was his job to dig the holes to make the warrens for the rabbits he would put down them. He would then look after the rabbits, thousands of them, feeding them and protecting them from foxes and poachers.

You see, a poacher is someone who hunts for animals that are not theirs. This is a big problem for someone like a warrener. Not only would the poachers try to catch the rabbits to sell them on themselves, but they would try to do away with the warrener so that they could steal as many rabbits as they could, night after night, and not worry about getting caught. Rabbits were big business, you see. Not only did people eat them but they used their furs in clothing and people paid good money for them. Because of this, the warrener had to be safe. His house had bars on the windows and turrets on the roof. It was more like a fortress than a home, but it kept the people inside safe from the poachers.

However, things changed in 1880 when the law changed. Now, farmers were allowed to shoot and kill rabbits on their own land, which they couldn't do before. With all the farmers selling the rabbits they had caught, rabbits were not worth as much and the warreners went out of business. This is what happened to the warrener of Thetford. He moved out and the house, with all its fortifications, went to ruin.

Little Tommy had been told stories of the great warrens of Thetford. He'd also been told of the White Rabbit, a ghostly beast thought to roam the lands with its glowing red eyes, searching for poachers or anyone who would do wrong to the rabbits of the warren. The other children thought it was nonsense and poppycock, but not Tommy. He wanted to believe it so much – it was such a great story! But, because he was the only one who believed it, the others often teased him. This day was no different.

'Hey, you're that kid who believes in the White Rabbit, aren't you?' came the shouts from the local bullies. 'I bet you believe in the Easter bunny too!' They began to nudge each other and laugh in a horrible way that made Tommy feel both upset and angry. The bullies walked towards Tommy. 'So, if he's real, where is he? Well?'

Tommy felt his blood begin to boil and his fist clench. Before he knew it, he had swung his right hand around and connected with the biggest of the three bullies' nose. It was like popping a water balloon filled with ketchup. Blood erupted EVERYWHERE! It felt amazing, teaching the bullies a lesson. Tommy felt on top of the world. Tommy felt amazing! Tommy felt … scared. He saw the three bullies standing in front of him, faces like thunder, one with added lava from the still erupting blood volcano on his face. 'Get him!' screamed the bully with the nosebleed.

Tommy turned and ran towards the tree line, his tormentors hot on his heels. Tommy was smaller than the bullies but just as fast, and he found nipping through the trees easier, so started to get a bit of a lead. That's when he saw it. The sun was setting and the light was draining from the land. As Tommy burst into a large clearing he saw it, a massive fort built from flint. This building had been built to last, for sure. Nobody lived in it any more, that was clear. Maybe Tommy could hide out in there!

Heading for the door, Tommy raced inside. Ducking and weaving in the almost complete darkness, he found a nook to crouch down in and hide. There he sat, there he waited, there he listened.

'Come out, you little nerd, we know you're in there,' said the voice of one of the bullies. No answer. They didn't want to admit it, but none of the three lads wanted to go in.

The darkness made them uneasy and, well, what if the stories were true?

Pushing and jostling each other, they eventually went in. Once their eyes adjusted to the gloom, they began to search. 'Come out, come out, wherever you are. Stop cuddling your bunny and come and get what you deserve.'

At that moment, Tommy heard them come into the room where he was hiding. He also heard another noise, like large padded feet getting closer. It couldn't be …

Into the room burst a huge white rabbit. The bullies were thrown backwards onto their behinds. That's when they saw it. The beast in front of them was the size of a small horse! It had matted white fur and skin so tight that every bone could be seen sliding about underneath. The head of the creature spun around, eyes of flame staring into the children's souls. All three bullies began to scream, a high pitched scream normally only heard coming from a young girl's mouth, not big, brutish bully-boys like them.

They scrambled for the door and were gone, their screams drifting off into the fading evening. The rabbit slowly began to fade away into thin air. Tommy watched as the last thing to go were the eyes, which turned suddenly and looked straight at him in his hiding spot. Tommy held his breath. The flaming eyes vanished and left him in the pitch black.

Where did this White Rabbit come from? What was his reason for being there in Thetford? Nobody quite knows, but next time you are in Thetford forest, beware of the White Rabbit – he might come for YOU!

The Legend of the Beast of Southery

I start this story off with a warning. If you don't like gruesome stories, tales of grizzly deaths or monstrous beasts, then skip ahead. If you do like all of this or are just feeling particularly brave, then read on, my friend. But, be warned, what is once read cannot be unread. Enjoy …

Back in the times when Thetford forest was a criss-cross of waterways and fens, and the village of Southery was an island in the middle of the great river Ouse, the monks of the local area came to build a church to spread the word of their god. The people of this island were simple folk, living in simple thatched huts, and using simple ways to catch eels and fish to live a simple life. They would also often rob the boats heading up and down the river from Cambridge to Ely, making this a truly treacherous stretch of the river. The monks knew they would have their work cut out for them, converting these people to a more righteous way of life.

It wasn't long after the monks' arrival on the island that some of them started to go missing, only to turn up no longer breathing. The monks' friends, rightly assuming that the locals had something to do with it, sent word to the abbot of Ely, who arranged for a troupe of guards to be stationed on the island to keep the peace. Well, that was a mistake. The local people didn't take kindly to the church wading in on their business, sending their guards to police the villagers' own island. The guards stayed for several weeks, their main task being to find out who had murdered the monks. This proved impossible as the locals kept their lips shut as tight as a jam jar (and we all know how hard it is to open a new jar of jam!).

The guards returned to the abbot of Ely empty handed and none the wiser. Desperate to keep his monks safe, the abbot asked the baron of Northwold, down the road in Norfolk, for help. Now, he did not send any men, as he had already lost a great deal to the bandits and robbers of that area, but he did have a pack of wild wolf-hounds. These were savage beasts, more wild wolf than dog. He sent these to guard the monks within the walls of the church they were building, but things were not going to go the way they expected.

When the wolf-hounds arrived, the monks tried to gain their trust and loyalty by feeding them. This, they were told, was the way to do it. The baron had assured them that as long as they fed the beasts, they would not attack the monks but would protect them with their lives. The monks turned out their pantries for the creatures, the finest fish and the freshest eels. This did not take the wolf-hounds' fancy. The alpha, the leader of the pack, sniffed the food. His nose wrinkled, his teeth, like daggers, appeared beneath curled lips, and he turned to pad slowly out of the church. With the leader of the pack leaving the fish, the rest followed suit. They disappeared out of the church and into the undergrowth on the island.

That night the monks sat and spoke about what had happened. Many of them were panicked by the wolf-hounds' departure and were sure nothing good would come of it. They all agreed to shut the doors and carry on building at speed, from the inside out, to try and complete the church as a safe haven. Word was also sent to the abbot for help.

For the first few weeks after the wolf-hounds left the church, all was quiet. Rarely were they seen by monk or villager, and when they were it was a flash of fur from one bush to another, so well camouflaged were their coats. You see, my friends, they had found food more to their liking. They had found the monks who had been killed and not discovered; they had found the villagers whom the guards had questioned until they lived no longer. The pack feasted on their flesh, banqueted on their bones.

But alas, the food slowly ran out and their stomachs became empty once more. They then turned their attention from the dead to the living. They would stalk the village at night, seeking ways into the huts of the villagers, taking them as they slept. Slowly the village emptied of people, some thanks to the wolf-hounds, most through fleeing in fear. When the huts were empty, the beasts turned their attention upon the church. Cracks were found, holes sniffed out and teeth sunk into monks. Eventually, the church too became empty, with most of the monks, like the villagers, choosing to flee rather than become dinner for the foul beasts they had failed to tame, creatures sent to protect them who now preyed on them.

With the island deserted, the food for the foul beasts ran dry. The creatures shunned the fast-flowing, wide waters of the Ouse and stayed on the island, as if in exile for what they had done. Before long, the hunger took them over and they began to turn on each other, one by one. It started with the smallest and weakest of the pack, but it soon came down to just two left, the alpha male and the alpha female. Both the fiercest in the pack, both driven mad with hunger.

When people finally dared to set foot back on the island, they were met with the sight of the remaining beast, the last of the pack of wolf-hounds that had hunted them out of their home. It was a female hound, weak, starving, nothing but skin and bones, clinging onto life. Too weak to have a say in what happened to her, she was taken in by a family, returning to their old home. The mother had not long had a baby, so she fed both her child and the weakened wolf-hound with her own milk. This gave it strength and, before long, the once-terrifying creature was now a tame pet, fully restored to health. The villagers heard news of this, that the island was safe, and so returned to their homes, and likewise, the monks returned to finish building the church. Enough blood had been shed between the villagers and the monks that they now lived in peace, the wolf-hound a constant reminder of what had happened and, now, the island's protector.

Life was good, the church not far from completion, when, one night, the wolf-hound went missing. The river was low for that time of the year and she had managed to swim the short distance to the far bank. Nearly two weeks later she returned, her paws cut and torn. The villagers could see she had travelled many, many miles. Over the coming days, the hound's belly began to swell and it was clear she was pregnant. She gave birth to just one cub, a cub the size of a small dog. This cub was no wolf-hound; his features were more like a domestic dog than a wolf. But he grew to a great height, some people reporting that he was the size of a donkey!

The day came when the wolf-hound mother passed away and her son took her place as protector of the village, seeing off anyone who would seek to do the villagers or the monks harm. The day also came when the church was finished and word was sent to the abbot of Ely. He soon arrived to bless the troubled building and rejoice in its completion. Arriving on horseback with an armed guard of several men, the abbot rode into the village to greet the people and the monks. He was greeted by the son of the wolf-hound, the village protector. Having heard of what the wolf-hounds had done all that time ago and worrying that this was a remnant of the pack, the abbot reached for his sword, ready to fend off the creature. If he had waited, the beast would have been soothed by the villagers and no harm would have come to the abbot. However, now the beast saw the man as a threat to his people. In a single, huge bound, the beast tore the abbot from his horse and saw to it that he would never take another breath.

The abbot's guards, acting in his defence, drew their bows and unleashed a volley of arrows into the creature, sending him bowling over, onto his side, dead. The villagers and the monks were united in their grief, the villagers for the loss of such a brave protector, the monks at the loss of their abbot and a loyal friend in the wolf-hound.

The beast was laid to rest on the same day, in a grave upon that island. The year is not known but the day was 29 May. It is said that, if you walk the fens, now the edge of the great Thetford forest, in the evening of 29 May each year, you may hear that faithful friend, protector of the people of Southery, howling to the moon, warning strangers to stay away. It is also said that, if you hear him, then you are doomed to die within the year, the great beast tracking you down for trespassing upon his master's lands.

Don't believe me? Go on, try it. I'll see you in Southery on 29 May and we can see if the beast of Southery has it in for us or if he thinks we are friends.

See, I told you this one was gruesome and grizzly, but I have to confess, I think it might be my favourite of the stories in this book.

DID YOU KNOW?

Pine forests are made up of evergreen pine trees, like Christmas trees. They grow fast and are great for making things out of. Their wood is soft but very useful. Pine trees are mostly found in colder regions, such as Scotland, the Alps and the Arctic Circle, where they grow well, despite the cold and snow. In these regions, people race through the pine forests on sleighs pulled by husky dogs. If there is no snow, the sleighs have wheels. Such races often happen in Thetford forest.

WHY DON'T YOU?

Go hunting for phantom beasts!
Keep your eyes out for tracks on
the ground. Can you tell what they
are? Are they particularly big? What
beast could they belong to? Where
do they go? How far can you follow
them? Look for soft mud, which gives
the best tracks to follow. Good luck
and remember, if you see a phantom
beast, my advice is RUN!!!

Robin Hood

Sherwood Forest

Time for you to listen, friend,
to a story often told,
Of a man, cast out from the law,
a man both brave and bold.
Of his deeds, the songs were sung
and many a story heard,
Then came books to keep them in
and store them in written word.
But let me tell you of a time,
before the men so merry,
Before the maid so fair, the monk
so fat and the John so hairy.
It may be true, it may be not,
but does thy really care,
For the story that I am about to
tell will give both a laugh and scare.

In a land ruled by a tyrant prince who wanted to be king, there stood one man against his rule. This man had been made an outlaw, cast out from society, a wanted man for the crimes the crown had said he'd committed. With his trusted band of followers, this man took from those who had too much and gave to those who needed it the most. His name became a legend within his own lifetime; he was a hero to the poor and a man to fear to the rich.

Of course, we all know this man by the name Robin Hood, and his trusted band of followers as his Merry Men, consisting of the giant of a man, Little John; the portly holy man, Friar Tuck; the brave but sometimes foolish Will Scarlett; Robin's one true love, the fair Maid Marion, and, the most important of them all, the bard, Allen-A-Dale. He was the one who sang the songs of Robin's brave deeds, who told the stories of the sacrifices Robin made for those less well off than himself and who spread the word of Robin's true story – an honest nobleman, cast down by the evil Prince John, stripped of all his lands and titles and now one of the common folk.

Robin of Loxley, some people say he was. A lord, an owner of land, a gentleman, who fought in the crusades alongside the one true king, King John, returned home only to be made a villain by Prince John and chased and hunted down by the Sheriff of Nottingham and his men.

The legends tell us of how Robin and his Merry Men hid in Sherwood Forest, of how they used the now famous Major Oak to hide from the sheriff and his men. They lived off the land, using what the forest gave them to survive. And the forest did not let them down. Everything from food to building materials could be found. After all, in those days, at the turn of the thirteenth century, the great forest of Sherwood was said to have stretched, unbroken, from the Yorkshire coast to the edge of Leicester.

You may well know many stories of Robin Hood, of how he met Little John on the log crossing a river, of how he rescued his men from the castle at Nottingham and of his daring attempt to win the golden arrow at the archery tournament in order to gain a kiss from his sweetheart, Maid Marion. But there is one story I am guessing you have not heard. This is a story that was told to me many years ago by a great storyteller from Nottingham, a man by the name of Pete Davis, a storyteller who, sadly, can no longer tell his stories as his time in this world was tragically cut short. I tell this story and write it here for you as a way of remembering him, just like Allen-A-Dale did to ensure we remembered Robin.

The story may not be totally true, but who cares? Folk tales always bend the rules, twist the facts, that's what makes them interesting! Robin Hood probably never was Robin of Loxley. The name Robin Hood was as common back then as John Smith is today. He could easily have been lots of different people whose stories have all been mashed together to create the legend we know, but what does it matter? We love a good story, and what I am about to tell you is one of those – I hope you agree.

Robin Comes to Sherwood

Back in the days when Robin had just been made an outlaw, he wandered the land, not knowing what to do with himself. No home, no money, just his faithful longbow, a quiver full of arrows, a leather satchel and his trusty knife. He wandered and wandered until he came to an inn, perched like a bird on the edge of the infamous Sherwood Forest. Robin entered, hoping he could cut a deal with the landlord for some food and drink in return for his hard labour, perhaps.

Robin struck up a conversation with the landlord and he offered to use the landlord's axe to go and chop some wood in the forest for his fire, as Robin had noticed the pile was getting small near the hearth.

'Ya don't wanna do that, that's madness!' replied the landlord in shock.

'Why ever not?' replied Robin in a very polite manner. 'It's a forest, a woodland full of trees and wood for fires, for crafting furniture and tools, and for building houses. Why would you not go in to collect some wood?'

The landlord looked shaken and confused. 'Have ya not 'eard about that place? 'Bout what's in there?'

Robin shook his head. The landlord began telling him. He told of an indescribable evil that had come to the forest some time ago and had begun to scare the forest folk away. The creature was huge. The people rarely stayed around to get a good look at it, choosing mostly to turn and flee out of the forest, vowing never to return.

'Well,' replied the young hero-to-be, 'somebody better do something about it.' And with that, Robin stood up and walked to the door with a wry grin on his face.

'Madness!' cried the landlord. 'Folly! Ya shan't come back, I tell ya!'

Ignoring the warning, Robin ventured into the forest, nothing but his bow, arrows, bag, knife and wits to help him. His feet carried him swiftly through the green wood for a little under half a day until he came to a clearing. Robin stopped and looked around. It was very odd. The clearing was totally man made. The woodsman had felled many a tree, some of great girth and good quality, with many strong and straight branches, but they all lay there still. It was not as if they had only just been chopped down, though. It was clear to Robin, by the way the tree stumps had dulled in colour, that these trees had been chopped down some time ago. But why had they been left? Had the great creature scared away the woodsman before he had the chance to take his hard work from the forest?

Robin decided this must be the case and, well, if the creature had come this way once before, maybe it would come this way again. Robin came up with a plan and began to carry it out. He took out an arrow from his quiver and sat himself down on a tree stump. Removing his knife from its sheath, he stripped the feathered fletchings from the arrow shaft. Then he snapped the metal bodkin point from the other end. He set about pretending to carve an arrow, in the way he had done for real, many, many times before with straight branches. As he pretended to work, Robin pursed his lips together and began to whistle a merry tune.

The sun carried on its journey across the sky, and the notes that left Robin's lips, notes as tuneful as the bird that shared his name, drifted through the trees and danced into the rather large ears of something nearby. This rather large something stood up and sniffed the air before listening once more. It then began to move.

As Robin sat and whistled, he heard a thumping noise, getting closer and closer. The closer it got, the more Robin could hear a second noise, that of the creaking of trees as if they were being blown about by a hugely powerful wind. Keeping his nerve, Robin kept his head down and continued pretending to carve.

Finally, into the clearing the large something came. Keeping his head bowed low,

Robin managed to strain his eyes upwards to spy the creature. To Robin's surprise, it was a man! But not just any man. This man was gigantic, standing as tall as some of the tallest trees. The other thing that made him different from normal men was that he had a single eye, positioned right in the middle of his forehead. A great green eye, staring crazed towards Robin. The giant cyclops, for that is what you call a creature with one eye, strode purposefully towards the strange little man who was sitting on the tree stump on the far side of the clearing.

'WHAT ARE YOU DOING IN MY FOREST?' bellowed the cyclops towards Robin. Robin could feel the heat of his breath and he could smell it. Boy, could he smell it! This cyclops obviously didn't know what a toothbrush was.

Robin was scared. No, Robin was petrified! He had to try hard not to react as this would break the illusion and the plan would fail. Instead of shaking, Robin just raised his hand, keeping his head lowered, and said, 'Hold on, would you? I'm nearly done.'

The cyclops took a step back! Who was this little man telling the cyclops to hold on? Nobody told the cyclops to hold on, especially in his forest, especially a scrawny little man like this! 'I said, WHAT ARE Y ...'

The cyclops was interrupted by a shushing noise and Robin placing his finger on his lips. Nobody had EVER done this to the cyclops! He didn't know what to do, other than do as he was told, so he stood patiently and waited.

After a minute or two, Robin sheathed the knife, returned the arrow shaft to the quiver and looked up. 'Sorry, I was just finishing off making that arrow. The trees that have been cut down here are perfect for them.' With that Robin smiled.

The cyclops look confused, his forehead as crinkled as screwed-up paper. 'But,' he stuttered, 'you don't make arrows from trees. You make them from thin branches, don't you?'

'Oh,' replied Robin without missing a beat, 'most normal people do, but I've found that the best wood for arrows comes from the centre heartwood of the main tree trunk. You see, I pick up a tree and use my magic knife to whittle it down to the thickness I need, and these trees are perfect for it! 'Robin finished with an unnerving smile towards the cyclops.

The cyclops was now a little scared. This little man could pick up AND carve down a whole tree! He must be impossibly strong. The cyclops didn't want to mess with him!

'So,' Robin continued, 'you said this was your forest, which makes me your guest …' The cyclops spluttered and stumbled to find some words but none came, so Robin continued. 'So therefore I feel that it's only polite that you invite me back to your dwelling and offer me some lunch and a drink. That's the polite thing to do for a guest and you wouldn't want to upset me, now would you?' The question was a tricky one for the cyclops. Did he dare to say no and risk getting beaten with a tree trunk by this impossibly strong little man? The answer was no.

'Oh, yes, of course, w-where are my manners?' came the stuttered reply. 'F-follow m-me.'

The cyclops led Robin through the forest, bending trees with his shovel-like hands as he went. Robin's heart raced and a bead of nervous sweat formed on his forehead, only to be swept quickly away by his sleeve. Before long, they arrived at a large wooden hut. It was made out of whole tree trunks stacked high with a roof covered in grass. Robin was impressed that what seemed like a rather simple creature had managed to build such an impressive house.

Robin was asked, politely, by the cyclops to take a seat on a tree stump near the front door. The cyclops mumbled, 'I have porridge in the pot. Would that be any good for lunch?' He squinted his single eye and winced in fear of the little man's response.

'That'll do nicely,' answered Robin, so into the house went the cyclops.

Moments later he reappeared, a bucket filled to the brim with porridge in one hand, and a normal-sized bowl of porridge in the other. Robin looked up with a puzzled expression. 'I do hope that bucket is for me and not the bowl. I'm very hungry, you know!'

'What?!' exclaimed the cyclops. He wondered where on earth the little man would fit a whole bucket of porridge. Surely his stomach wasn't big enough but, then again, the cyclops hadn't expected that this little man could make arrows out of a tree! 'Oh, no, erm, I, erm … hold on …' The cyclops lolloped back inside, only to emerge once more with two full buckets.

The cyclops handed one to Robin and took one for himself. Robin raised his hand and said, 'After you, my friend.'

Not wanting to argue with this terribly strange yet terribly strong little man, the cyclops lifted his bucket and began to eat, the only way a giant cyclops knows how. He buried his head in the bucket, closing his eye for fear of getting sticky porridge in it. He slurped and burped his way to the bottom, with bits of stray porridge sliding down his chin towards the floor.

Robin, on the other hand, drew round his leather satchel, opened it wide and emptied the contents of the bucket into it, before closing it up and concealing it under his shirt so as to make it look like he had a full belly. Robin then let out a whopping great 'BUUUUURRRRRRPPPPPP!'

The cyclops froze. He opened his single eye and peered over the rim of the bucket to see that Robin had an empty bucket and a full stomach. 'Ha-have you f-finished al-already?' tripped the question out of his mouth.

'I have,' came the response, 'and it was so good I would love a top-up. Another bucket of porridge, if you would, my kind host?'

What could the cyclops do? This little man could lift a tree, whittle it down to an arrow, eat a whole bucket of porridge in seconds AND have room for more! The cyclops had never been so scared of anyone in his life! 'Of course, sir, right away, sir, it's coming now, sir …'

With that, the cyclops produced two refilled buckets of porridge, one for Robin and one for himself (well, he couldn't let his guest eat and not eat himself, thought the cyclops, that would just be rude!). Once more the cyclops was told to start first and once more he buried his head in the bucket, closing his eye tight shut. Once more – yes, readers, you guessed it – Robin opened his satchel and emptied the porridge into it, before closing it and hiding it under his shirt.

'BUUUUUUUUUUUUURRRRRRRR RRRRRRRRRRRPPPPPPPPPPPPPPPP PPPPP!'

The trees shook with the sound of the air rushing from Robin's mouth. 'That was lovely, as good as the first bucket for sure.' With Robin's remark, the cyclops stopped and peered over the bucket rim to spy a very fat little man with a very large grin on his face. 'I don't suppose you have a bucket of water I could wash this down with, do you? And get one for yourself.'

The cyclops said not a word. He dropped his porridge bucket and ran inside, appearing seconds later with the buckets of water that he'd been asked for. 'After you,' came the response from Robin once he'd received his bucket.

The cyclops drank the water in much the same, revolting way he had eaten the porridge, his whole face buried and his eye closed, water gushing down his chin and onto his chest, causing his white shirt to go see-through, exposing his grizzly hairy chest beneath.

What do you think Robin did? Do you think this wily fox drank it? Of course not, you're right. Robin threw the contents out over his shoulder and, for a third time …

'BUUUUUUUUUUUUUUUUURRRR RRRRRRRRRRRRRRRRRRRRRRRRP PPPPPPPPPPPPPPPPPPPPPPPPP!'

This burp was so long and so loud that people in Nottingham heard the rumbling and stopped what they were doing.

The cyclops peered over the bucket rim for the third time, his eye filled with fear and terror. What was this creature in front of him? He was no man!

'Thank you,' said Robin. 'That was so lovely, that porridge, that I would very much like a third bucketful, if it's not too much trouble?'

The cyclops' jaw hit the floor. Astonishment winning out over fear, he spoke freely. 'That is impossible. I don't mean to upset you, but how on this very earth can you fit any more in there?' He pointed to Robin's stomach: 'It's full to bursting!'

Robin stood up and smiled. 'Simple – by doing this with my magic knife.'

Robin drew his knife, pulled his shirt forward and inserted the knife into the bottom of the leather satchel. He drew the knife from one end of the satchel to the other and all the porridge flopped out onto the floor.

'There, magic! My stomach is empty, my wounds are healed, I'm fine and ready for more.' Robin's smile stretched from ear to ear.

The cyclops was astounded, dumbstruck, in total amazement at what he had just witnessed. Without even thinking, the cyclops asked, 'Can I have a go?'

'Of course you can,' replied Robin. 'Here you go.'

Robin watched as the cyclops took the knife, which looked like a needle in his huge hands, lifted up his shirt, dug the dagger deep into his hairy belly and slit it open from one side to the other. All of a sudden, the cyclops twitched as a bolt of pain shot up his spine and watched all his insides became outsides. The cyclops had just enough time to look Robin in the eye and say, 'Hey, you tricked me! That's not f …' before he fell to the floor, stone cold dead!

Robin returned to the inn and to the landlord, and told him of his adventure. Robin was hailed as a hero by all. The village in which this inn sat was Oxton and, if you walk to the north of Oxton, you will find a hill. Some say this is an ancient hill fort from the iron age but we know differently, don't we? You see, where that giant cyclops fell, over the years, grass took over his body and hid his house, creating the mound you can see today. The hill is even called Robin Hood Hill after our hero's brave deed. Sherwood Forest, or what is left of it, can now be found north of here. Next time you are venturing into the greenwood, remember, Robin Hood not only fought men but also the odd monster too.

DID YOU KNOW?

The Major Oak, Robin Hood's hiding place, is thought to be nearly 1,000 years old! And it is still alive!

Each year, around the new Sherwood Forest visitor centre and throughout the forest itself, a festival is held in the great man's honour. The Robin Hood festival brings Robin Hood, his Merry Men, Maid Marion, the Sheriff of Nottingham and all the other characters of the legends to life, alongside musicians, storytellers and many more things to see.

If you can't get to the festival, the new visitor centre is the perfect place to start your adventure around the greenwood. You never know, you might catch a glimpse of the man in tights himself, if you're lucky!

WHY DON'T YOU?

Get together a band of merry men and go and explore your local forest. Make swords and bows and arrows from sticks and string. Maybe you could find a log and pretend to be Robin and Little John when they first met on the river crossing. Can you get past each other without either of you falling off? I would suggest you do this on a log on the ground, not over a river or stream, just in case you do fall off. You wouldn't want to be walking around with soggy pants all day, now would you?!

Witches and Wizards

Forest of Dean

'Double, double, toil and trouble',
famously they spoke,
As round the cauldron, these three
gathered and the magic they awoke,
But deep within the woods, they hide,
the sisters, brothers of the night,
Seeking to bring eternal darkness,
extinguishing the light.
Casting spells and making curses,
changing shape and form,
Their bodies twist, their bodies writhe,
their bodies start to deform.
Do not cross them, leave them be,
let them well alone,
Never mean to upset them or
invite them into your home.

Stretching across the border of England and Wales, from Gloucestershire to Monmouthshire, lies one of the country's last remaining ancient forests and royal hunting grounds. Known as the Forest of Dean, this wooded area was even bigger back in medieval times than it is now. The forest is truly a magical place, with many wondrous places to visit, such as Puzzlewood, with its strange landscapes, twisted trees and endless places to explore. So it is no wonder that many tales of strange goings-on and old beliefs lasted a lot longer here than in many other places in the country. One common belief was in witches. The people of the forest believed these to be mostly women (but not always, as you will see), out to cause harm to the good folk of the land, using magic they had gained through making a pact with the Devil – Old Scratch or Old Nick as he was often called in folklore. Along with this fear of witches and wizards came many stories of their strange powers, such as the ones I am about to tell you.

Jack-o-Kent and the Devil

There once was a young man who lived on the border of England and Wales, in amongst the green leaves and the boughs of the Forest of Dean. Many stories are told of him and his dealings with the Devil, for that is from whom he got his power. He possessed great magic and greater strength and used these many times to outsmart Old Nick.

One year the Devil, keen to finally outsmart Jack, came to him and made a deal. He said to Jack that he would ensure the perfect weather for growing the perfect crop and, in return, Jack was to give the Devil either the top or bottom of the plants as payment, but the Devil would choose.

Old Scratch thought he was smart and chose the top, as when wheat and barley grow, the bit you use is collected from the top of the stem. This would leave Jack with the useless stems beneath, good for nothing but scratchy straw. However, when Jack was told this he planted turnips. They grew fat in the ground and, come harvest, the Devil was presented with the tops, a pile of useless leaves!

Not happy about being outsmarted, the Devil insisted on the same deal next year and chose the bottoms. This time, however, Jack planted wheat and this meant he collected the harvest all for himself, leaving Old Nick with the scratchy straw.

On another occasion, the Devil challenged the mighty Jack-o-Kent to a stone-throwing contest to test the strength that he had given the man. He felt certain he was still stronger than Jack. They both stood in Trelleck, north of the river Severn, and both chose huge boulders.

The Devil went first. His throw was impressive, flying through the air and landing 2.4km away in Stroat. In fact, if you go there even to this day, you can find the stone he threw, a stone known as the Broadstone or the Devil's Quoit. The Devil was happy with what he had done and sat back to watch Jack's feeble attempt.

Jack picked a stone of the same size, lifted it above his head with one hand and hurled it over the forest, over the river Severn and on into Thornbury, some 5km away, twice as far as the Devil. With a face like thunder and full of rage, the Devil disappeared in a puff of smoke. Jack had won this day but there would be more challenges to come, that was for sure.

The Witches of Whitebrook

As I have said, people in the Forest of Dean still believed in witches long after the rest of the country had moved on and left those fears behind. As late as 1902, stories of witchcraft were still being reported.

There was once a woman who was walking through the forest, minding her own business, when out from behind a bush emerged an old hag. She was hunched over so much that her head was level with her knees and her back arched like a bridge. She wore a tatty old hooded cloak that hid her face, for the most part; just a long, crooked nose peered out from underneath. Heavily she leaned upon a gnarled old stick and hobbled towards the woman.

'My dearest,' said the hag, her voice like metal work being dragged down the street, 'my dearest, come, help an old woman out, would you? Be a dear.'

Being kind-hearted and of good nature, the woman hurried over to the hag to assist her. When she got there, she took her by the arm as if to help her on her way.

'No, no, no!' The hag's voice pierced the forest stillness. 'I don't mean like that. I'm perfectly capable of walking without you – I need the money that is in your purse, hanging from your belt. That will buy me just what I need.'

The woman took a step back. This old hag wasn't joking. She was now looking up from beneath her hood and the woman could see that her skin was pale and covered in warts, her hair was dank, patchy and lifeless, and her eyes were different colours, one grey and one a brilliant blue. The woman clutched her purse tightly and spoke. 'Forgive me, but this is my money that I have worked hard for and I shall not part with it to you. Good day.' She turned and began to walk briskly away when the old hag started to speak.

'A curse on you, a curse I say, that all your cows will run away. Gone from you, gone they'll be and never again those beasts you'll see.'

A curse. That all made sense. This old hag, the crooked nose, the warts – this was a witch! The woman had upset a witch and now she had been cursed. However, the woman couldn't help but have a sneaky smile creep onto her face as the witch turned and hobbled off out of site, muttering the curse over and over under her breath. You see, the woman had no cows, so how could she lose them? This curse would not affect her in any way, she thought, so she brushed off the encounter and carried on with her day.

Everything was normal after that for the woman, for a while anyway. But slowly she began to get the feeling that she was forgetting something. That feeling you get when you leave the house and you think you've forgotten something, but you're not quite sure what it is, until you get to the car and realise it is the car keys, or your bag, or even your own head. Have you ever had that? I know I have.

This feeling began to grow stronger and stronger over the coming weeks, until one morning the woman found herself leaving her house, entering the woods and calling out for her cows. As we know, she had no cows, and the locals knew this too. They brought her back to her house, sat her down and explained this to her. The woman snapped back to her senses and began to explain what had happened with the witch some weeks ago.

The locals looked at each other, worry etched on their faces. They knew this curse would eat away at the woman and send her mad, but the only way to reverse the curse was to find the witch who did it and get her to lift it. A forest-wide search was conducted with all the villagers trying to help. They searched for days and days but no hag could be found. It was as if she had disappeared.

The woman, meanwhile, became more and more agitated. She was locked into her own house for fear that she would wander off. The woman would sit in the corner, rocking, wailing for her cows and how she needed to find them. Through all of this, a large nutbrown hare, with black tips on its ears, kept watch at a distance from the woman's house.

At length the people searched for the witch but, having had no luck, they finally gave up. Then, one day, driven mad by the curse, the woman managed to break out of her house and disappeared into the forest, calling her long-lost, non-existent cows at the top of her voice. And, as far as anyone knows, she still wanders the forest, even now, looking for her bovine friends. So, next time you are in the Forest of Dean, keep your eyes open and your ears sharp, for you may see that poor woman still searching for the cows she never had, thanks to the witch whom she wronged all those years ago.

Hare Today, Gone Tomorrow

Many stories are told of witches changing into animals, a process called transmogrification, and you might think it is mostly cats that witches turn into, but you'd be wrong. One of the most common forms for a witch to take, or so it is believed, is that of a hare, the larger cousin of the rabbit. Wait, haven't we already come across a hare in this chapter? Now it all makes sense!

Anyway, as we discovered in our first story, it's not just witches who are famed to live in the Forest of Dean, but wizards and warlocks, the men with magic, who live there too. They have all the same powers as the witches and this next short story proves it.

In Elton, on what was the far eastern side of the forest many years ago, there lived a very beautiful girl. She had come of age to marry and many a man had travelled far and wide to win her hand, but her father was, like most fathers, very protective of his little girl. He thought no man would ever be good enough for her and, having a daughter myself, I know exactly how he felt.

This being said, nobody can control whom another person falls in love with. Love just happens, no explanation why or how, love is love and when it hits it's powerful, more powerful than any magic. And it had hit the girl. There was a local lad, tall, not the best looking but with a smile that warmed the girl's heart and made her melt inside.

The father was worried that they had been meeting up without him knowing. He was also worried that there had been rumours that this lad was not quite what he seemed. It was said that he had been seen with certain older women, women thought to be into the dark arts, women thought to be witches. So, one Sunday morning, the father of the girl watched the lad go about his business. He saw him walking down the road to the church at Flaxley. This was good. A wizard or warlock would not go to church and, if he was at church, he wouldn't be with his daughter.

The father decided to go home and return to spy on the boy when the church service ended. Then he noticed a movement out of the corner of his eye. He saw, coming from the direction in which the lad had just walked, a large brown hare. From inside his house, the father watched the hare sitting opposite, looking at the house, and he grew suspicious. Could this be the lad in the form of a creature, using magic to change himself? He had to be sure, so he fetched out his bow and arrows. Still concealed in the darkness of his house and aiming out of the window, the father loosed an arrow into the hare's back right leg. The hare bolted as fast as he could into the bushes and disappeared.

The next day, the father's fears were confirmed, or so it seemed. He saw the lad, walking down the street, and he was walking with a limp, occasionally clutching at his right leg which looked to be bandaged and bloody.

A coincidence? Was he a wizard? What do you think? It's time for you to decide. We don't know what happened after that, but can only guess.

DID YOU KNOW?

You can time travel in the Forest of Dean. If you go to Littledean and find the church tower, at 11 o'clock you will find yourself 2 hours back in the past, only to hurtle back to the current time when the clock strikes 12. How is this possible? You might well ask. Well, if you look carefully at the clock face, you will see that the roman numeral for 11 has been painted as IX. In Roman numerals, this actually means 10 minus 1, making 9. For 11 it would be XI or 10 plus 1. Standing stones, such as the Broadstone in the Jack-o-Kent story, are very common in the Forest of Dean. Longstone, Buckstone, Toad's Mouth and the Harold Stones are all thought to date back to the Bronze and Iron ages, when the people of the land would move these stones great distances on wooden rollers and haul them into holes in the ground. Although we now have stories like that of Jack and the Devil to explain why they are there, we actually think the people who put them there did it to mark religious festivals or special times of the year.

WHY DON'T YOU?

Find an interesting stick to use as your wand and have a magical wand battle. What creatures could you turn into? Pretend to be a super-speedy hare or a clever old fox or even a hoppy frog. Keep an eye out for hares or other creatures watching you. Maybe they are witches and wizards in disguise!

Trees

The National Forest

What once was black, now is green,
The beauty that had gone unseen,
The trees return, they march on through,
They bring such joy to me and you.
The mines, the furnace, the engines gone,
A legacy that will live on,
Through buildings that crumble,
iron that rusts,
The old factories turned to dust.
Replaced by trees, all sizes, all kinds,
The oak, the ash grow above the mines.
And with their return come the birds,
The animals, the farms, the herds,
The stories, the lore, the peace and calm,
Nature returning the place from harm.

The National Forest is by far the newest of the forests in this book, but that does not mean it lacks folk stories. This being said, the folk tales are of the people and not the forest as the trees only began to take over the land in the 1990s. Before this, the area of the National Forest was awash with industry. Beneath the ground was found what became the blood of the industrial revolution in this country, coal. This coal would keep the fires burning, power the new steam engines and drive the country to greatness across the world, leading to the invention of canals, trains and eventually cars, to name but a few things. To get at the coal and other materials, such as iron ore, that were to be found deep underground, the land was either drilled into and hollowed out from underneath in deep mine shafts or scarred from above by great open-cast mines. Industry sprouted all around from mills to blast furnaces, like the one that still stands at Moira today, the best remaining example of an iron blast furnace.

All manner of things were produced and shipped across the country on the canals and railways, and across the world on new metal steam-powered ships.

With all of this industry, the trees, the forests and the woods were cut down faster than ever before, their wood being used to help destroy even more woodland. The once green landscape turned black from coal mines, factories and air thick with smoke. The old ways began to be lost as the people moved into cities and away from the countryside to get jobs. They worked every hour of the day to pay the bills and put food on their plate. They forgot how to live off the land, they forgot the stories of their ancestors, and they forgot the trees and the land on which they lived, for they spent too much time inside the land and not upon it as they had been before.

Since the 1990s and the creation of the National Forest, the land has slowly been transformed. Trees have been planted by the thousands to return the landscape from black to green. So, in honour of the trees being planted, I shall dedicate this chapter to the trees themselves and the folklore that lives within them.

The Mighty Oak

Considered by many to be the king of trees, the oak tree is thought to be the tree of the gods by civilisations across the world. In this country, we often find mistletoe growing amongst its branches, which not only comes in handy if you want a kiss at Christmas from that girl or boy you have fancied all year, but was also the most important plant for the Celtic druids. This meant the oak became a sacred place.

Stories around the oak are often found. One such story goes like this.

The year was warming up. The sun shone for many hours each day, the rain came and went when it was needed and the plants grew fat with fruit. Life on the land was good. The people grew even fatter than the plants, enjoying the bounty of nature. The mighty Oak sat upon the throne, ruling the land, the weather and its people. But although life was good, not everyone was happy. The Holly was plotting to take the Oak's throne. Long now he had waited. Many months the Holly had spent building up his strength, until the day came when the sun shone for its longest and night was but a fleeting whisper. The Holly gathered his might and launched an attack upon the Oak. Caught off guard and weak after many months of ruling, despite putting up a very valiant fight, the Oak lost.

The Holly now sat upon the throne and ruled the land. The Oak left, struggling to regain his strength. He waited the rest of the summer out in the sun before he shed his leaves, planted his acorns and began to plot his revenge.

This would come during the dead of winter, when the nights surrounded the day, giving the feeling that the sun had barely been able to come out. When the snow lay thick on the ground, the Oak took his chance. The Holly was growing fat on festive cheer, with the celebration of mid-winter. Overpowering the Holly, the Oak regained the throne. From there, he slowly brought back the sun, the warmth and the summer. He regrew his leaves and the cycle of the year continued, as it still does to this day, the Oak and the Holly locked in an on-going battle for the throne of the seasons.

Of course, we have already come across one of our country's most famous oaks, the Major Oak in Sherwood Forest, used by none other than Robin Hood to hide from the sheriff and his men. The oak is a symbol of strength and wisdom and can live for many hundreds of years.

Birch

The birch tree is an elegant thing, its white bark making it jump out of the woods as you look on. In folklore it is known as the lady of the woods. There are many tales that tell of the birch transforming into a beautiful woman, some thinking her to be Frigga or Freya, goddesses from the old ways, the Norse ways.

The birch's wispy, thin branches made it the perfect tree to use to make brooms. They were tied to the ends of thicker branches and these brooms were used not only to clean, but to brush away evil spirits from your house.

Again, we have come across some in this book who are famous for using these broomsticks. Witches are often thought to take flight on birch broomsticks, flying around the forests, searching for the ingredients for their potions.

Did you know that you can get a drink from a birch tree? In early spring, as the sap begins to rise in the waking tree, a tap can be driven into the birch trunk and a bucket left underneath. The sap will drain out of the tree and gather in the bucket. This can then be drunk as cordial or fermented to make wine.

Scots Pine

Pines and all evergreens are fast growing and their greenery lasts all year round. Because of this, they make great trees to plant if you want to replace a forest that has been recently chopped down. Can you think of one we may already have read about?

Up in Scotland, the ancient druids considered glades within pine forests as sacred places. They would decorate them during the winter solstice (the shortest day of the year) with lights, possibly made from pine cones filled with pine resin which, once lit, would burn brightly for a long time like a candle. They also used other decorations, and much celebration and dancing would occur. Do you remember the faeries from earlier on? Where did they dance and sing? That's right, in the glade of a pine forest! Also, decorating a pine tree in winter – does that sound familiar?

Ash

The mighty ash tree is thought to be able to cure many health problems for children. If a child was born with weak arms or legs, they would be passed through a cleft or hole made in an ash tree. The hole would then be tied back up to heal as the child's weak limbs also healed. Because of this, people also thought that the life of the child and the life of the tree were now linked, so when the child grew up, they would protect and look after that tree, believing that if it was cut down and died, they too would die.

Ash is one of the oldest species of trees, being found in many ancient forests. Much of the New Forest is made up of ash. It is useful for making tools and weapons out of, thanks to its straight growth and strength. This also makes it good for burning as it burns on a fire for a very long time. It was often used as a yule log, the log burned during Christmas celebrations.

Yew

The yew tree is amongst the longest-living trees known to man. There is a yew tree in north Wales, not far from where the dragons lived in my previous stories, that is thought to be upwards of 5,000 years old! This tree is in a place called Llangernyw, Conwy. If you are in the area, go and check it out!

Yew trees have been as important to this country as the oak. Oak trees built our ships, allowing us to discover and conquer the world; yew trees gave us the weapon to do this. The outer wood of a yew tree doesn't like to be stretched and, if it is, wants nothing more than to pull itself back to how it was. The inner heart wood is the opposite, not wanting to be squashed. This is the perfect combination for a bow. With the outer wood on the outside of the bow getting stretched and the heart wood on the inside getting squashed, the bow produces tremendous power.

The arrows shot from a longbow made of yew could pierce armour. These yew longbows, made and used by Welshmen, were the reason King Henry V won the Battle of Agincourt in 1415. The English army of 8,500 men (7,000 of them being archers) took on and beat 50,000 French soldiers. The English longbowmen filled the sky with arrows, completely destroying the French army before they could even get close to the English. All this thanks to the humble yew.

Just one warning, though: both the berries and needle leaves are deadly poisonous, so DO NOT eat them and always wash your hands after playing on or around a yew tree.

DID YOU KNOW?

There are many, many types of tree in this country but not all of them are native. Lots have come over from other countries. Can you find out what trees near you are from this country (native) and which ones are foreign?

National companies and trusts such as the Forestry England and the Woodland Trust have lots of resources to help you do this. Why don't you check them out?

WHY DON'T YOU?

Find, download and print off a tree identification chart. Then you can take this with you the next time you are out and about exploring. What trees grow near you? What trees grow in your local forests and woodlands? If they are not mentioned in this chapter, can you find any folklore about those trees to share with your friends?

The
Greenman

All Forests

There once was a small forest, a wooded island of calm and tranquillity, perched on the side of a hillside near a peaceful village. The woodland was well used and well loved by all the villagers. A teacher from the local primary school would often take his class up there to wander under the leafy canopy, to sketch the branches and study the life within this wonderland. A local historian frequented the site, for he believed this was once a place of great importance. He dug many small trenches, found many small finds and began to draw up his ideas. A naturalist, studying the flora and fauna of the local area, found himself drawn back to this forest time and time again, each time finding something new and exciting. The forest was perfect, magical.

One day, the villagers noticed a sign go up at the entrance to the forest. It was from the local council informing people of an application for planning permission. A large development company had bought the land on which the small woodland sat and planned to rip it up and build an estate of large houses, fit for the rich, the type of people who lived in the countryside at night but worked in the city by day.

A meeting was to be held at the village hall to discuss this application and the locals had their chance to put across their reasons why the plans should not go ahead – but, well, why would they be listened to, they thought. This was a multinational company worth billions of pounds. What they wanted they would get, surely. They could afford the best lawyers; the villagers arguing against them didn't stand a chance.

Even so, the meeting went ahead. It was a warm, early summer's evening. The sun was still shining bright but low in the sky as the teacher ran from his classroom and into the village hall, a pile of books still under his arm to be marked that night at home. There too, amongst the villagers, were the historian and the naturalist, but as both believed this was a foregone conclusion and that, no matter what they tried to say, they wouldn't win this fight, they had decided to keep quiet.

At the top table sat the businessmen and lawyers in their fancy suits, with the arbitrator, the man tasked with making the final decision, sitting in the middle. However, the villagers noticed there was someone else in the room. The funny thing was that they couldn't see them. This person seemed to be just out of sight, no matter where they looked. They could feel their presence but could not see them. They did not feel threatened by this person but calmed and reassured. The meeting began.

It started with the businessmen and the lawyers of the development company putting across their reasons for the development, something about the need for more housing in rural areas and meeting quotas set down by the government, all of which seemed very complicated to the villagers and didn't once address whether it was the right thing to do or not, just that they thought it should be done.

When they had finished, the arbitrator threw the meeting open to the audience for their opinions. It was silent. Then, with the doors and windows shut, a gust of air blew through the hall. It whipped up the teacher's class books and dropped them on the desk of the arbitrator. The room was confused and watched on as he looked at the work. He saw beautiful drawings, read finely crafted poems and mused over detailed studies of plants and animals, and he began to smile.

The historian felt a gentle warm breath on his ear and a warming inside. He suddenly felt himself rise to his feet and begin to speak. He told everyone there about his findings, of ancient artefacts and earthworks and how he believed the forest held the key to an undiscovered ancient settlement. If only he had more time and more resources, he could prove this, he pleaded. Having said his piece, he sat down, amazed at how eloquent and knowledge-able he had sounded. He smiled.

Suddenly, up sprang the naturalist. He too, like the historian, did not quite know what was happening, but had felt a warm, calming breeze in his ear and was filled with confidence. He began to talk about the rare plants he had found, an orchid and a fern found nowhere else in the county. He then spoke about the rare species of bat and butterfly living within the ancient trees in the forest and how they would be wiped out if the trees and the rest of the habitat were destroyed. The passion was clear in his voice, as it had been for the historian.

Once the naturalist had sat down, the rest of the villagers found a confidence they did not know they had. One after another they all said their piece. The sun had long since set and the night was drawing late when the caretaker finally turned off the lights and locked up the village hall. The arbitrator left with a lot to think over and a handful of school books he had asked to borrow to help him make up his mind.

The next morning, he sat in his garden surrounded by trees. He had the evidence for and against the new development in front of him, the school books, the notes he had taken of the points the villagers had raised and the very glossy, official-looking paperwork from the development company, and he began to think it over. As he did so, as was the case the night before, he felt he was not alone in that garden. He felt there was someone just out of sight, watching and guiding him.

Finally, the verdict was ready. An extraordinary meeting was called a few days later at the village hall and the arbitrator announced he would not be letting the development go ahead. The site was too important to build houses on and he was certain the development company could find a more suitable location. The cheers from the villagers almost took the roof off the village hall. The schoolchildren were given the next day off school to spend playing in and enjoying the woodland. The village had won a major battle.

As the champagne was being popped and the celebrations started, the teacher, historian and naturalist noticed someone leaving the hall. It was not one of the suits – they had all left in a huff immediately after the verdict had been given – but someone dressed head to toe in green. This man turned to the celebrating people and they could see now his face, kindly and smiling, his skin a deep verdant green, framed by a wreath of oak leaves. He placed his finger upon his lips and winked before disappearing on the wind.

This was the Greenman. He is the spirit of the forest, of nature itself. He walks the greenwoods looking after the birds, the beasts, the plants and the trees. It is he who looks after the fantastical creatures of folktale and myth and fills our hearts with joy and adventure when we enter his land.

The Greenman is everlasting but needs to be looked after in return. We need to fight for him and his realm. The forests and woodland will not be around forever unless we help him. Keep your eyes open, for on old buildings his face can still be seen, watching over the world, ensuring the safety of all those who live in it, and ensuring that we will always have our forests and woodland to explore and find peace in.

Bibliography

Rosemary Gray, *Scottish Myths and Legends*, Broxburn: Lomond Books, 2015.

Meirion Hughes and Wayne Evans, *Rumours and Oddities from North Wales*, Llanrwst: Gwawg Carred Gwalch, 1995.

Jennifer Westwood and Jacqueline Simpson, *The Lore of the Land*, London: Penguin, 2006.

Society *for*
Storytelling

Since 1993, The Society for Storytelling has championed the ancient art of oral storytelling and its long and honourable history – not just as entertainment, but also in education, health, and inspiring and changing lives. Storytellers, enthusiasts and academics support and are supported by this registered charity to ensure the art is nurtured and developed throughout the UK.

Many activities of the Society are available to all, such as locating storytellers on the Society website, taking part in our annual National Storytelling Week at the start of every February, purchasing our quarterly magazine Storylines, or attending our Annual Gathering – a chance to revel in engaging performances, inspiring workshops, and the company of like-minded people.

You can also become a member of the Society to support the work we do. In return, you receive free access to Storylines, discounted tickets to the Annual Gathering and other storytelling events, the opportunity to join our mentorship scheme for new storytellers, and more. Among our great deals for members is a 30% discount off titles from The History Press.

For more information, including how to join, please visit

www.sfs.org.uk